To Rosemary

How Dogs Really Work!

by · Alan · Snow

Little, Brown and Company

Boston Toronto London

First U.S. Edition

First published in Great Britain by HarperCollins Publishers Ltd.

ISBN 0-316-80261-1
Library of Congress Catalog Card Number 92-54651
Library of Congress Cataloging-in-Publication information is available.

10 9 8 7 6 5 4 3 2 1
Printed in Great Britain by BPCC Paulton Books Ltd.

This book is set in Snow Pirate Some Serif.

Contents

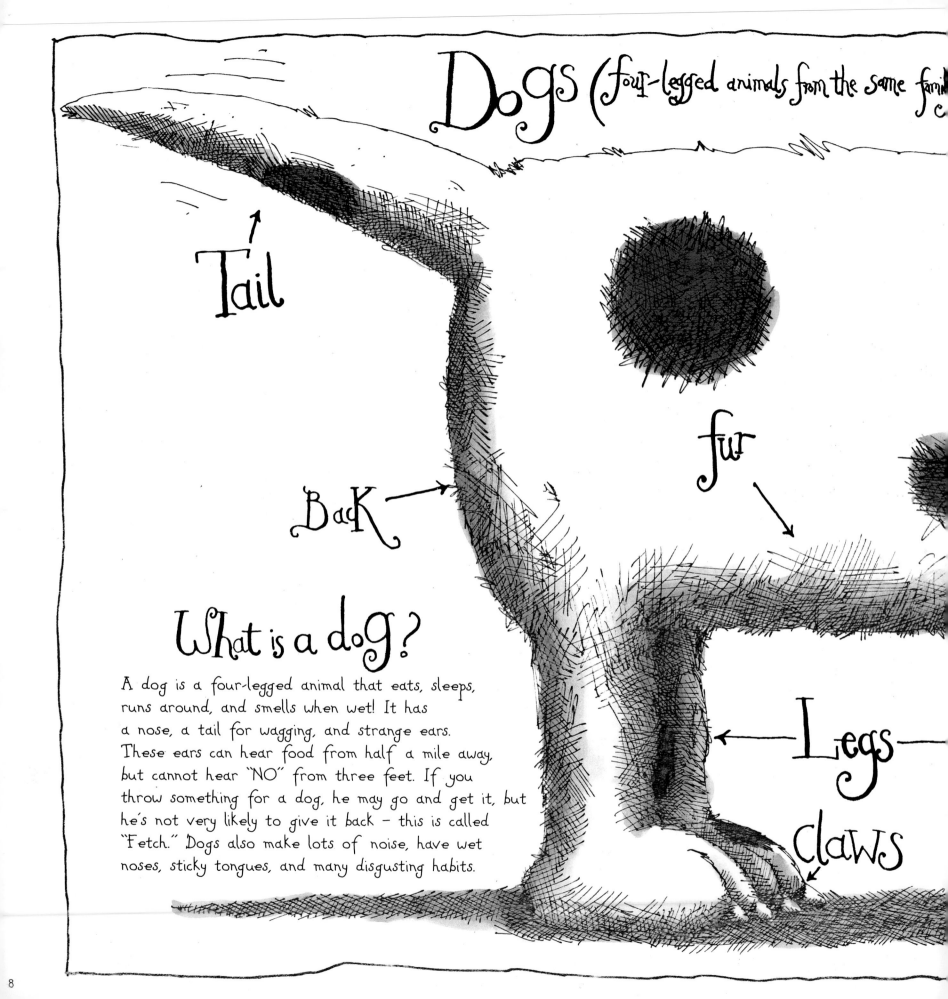

Dogs (four-legged animals from the same famil...

Tail

Back

fur

Legs

Claws

What is a dog?

A dog is a four-legged animal that eats, sleeps, runs around, and smells when wet! It has a nose, a tail for wagging, and strange ears. These ears can hear food from half a mile away, but cannot hear "NO" from three feet. If you throw something for a dog, he may go and get it, but he's not very likely to give it back – this is called "Fetch." Dogs also make lots of noise, have wet noses, sticky tongues, and many disgusting habits.

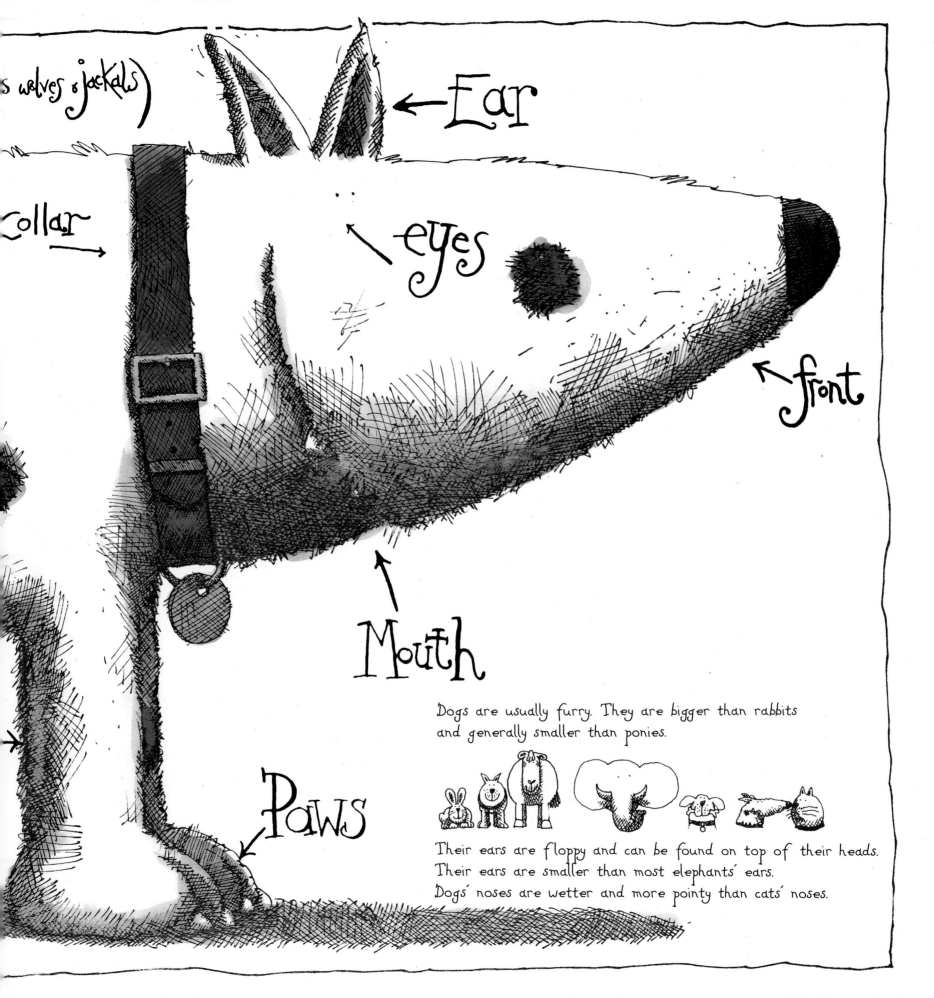

s wolves & jackals)

collar →

← Ear

eyes

← front

collar →

Mouth

Paws

Dogs are usually furry. They are bigger than rabbits and generally smaller than ponies.

Their ears are floppy and can be found on top of their heads.
Their ears are smaller than most elephants' ears.
Dogs' noses are wetter and more pointy than cats' noses.

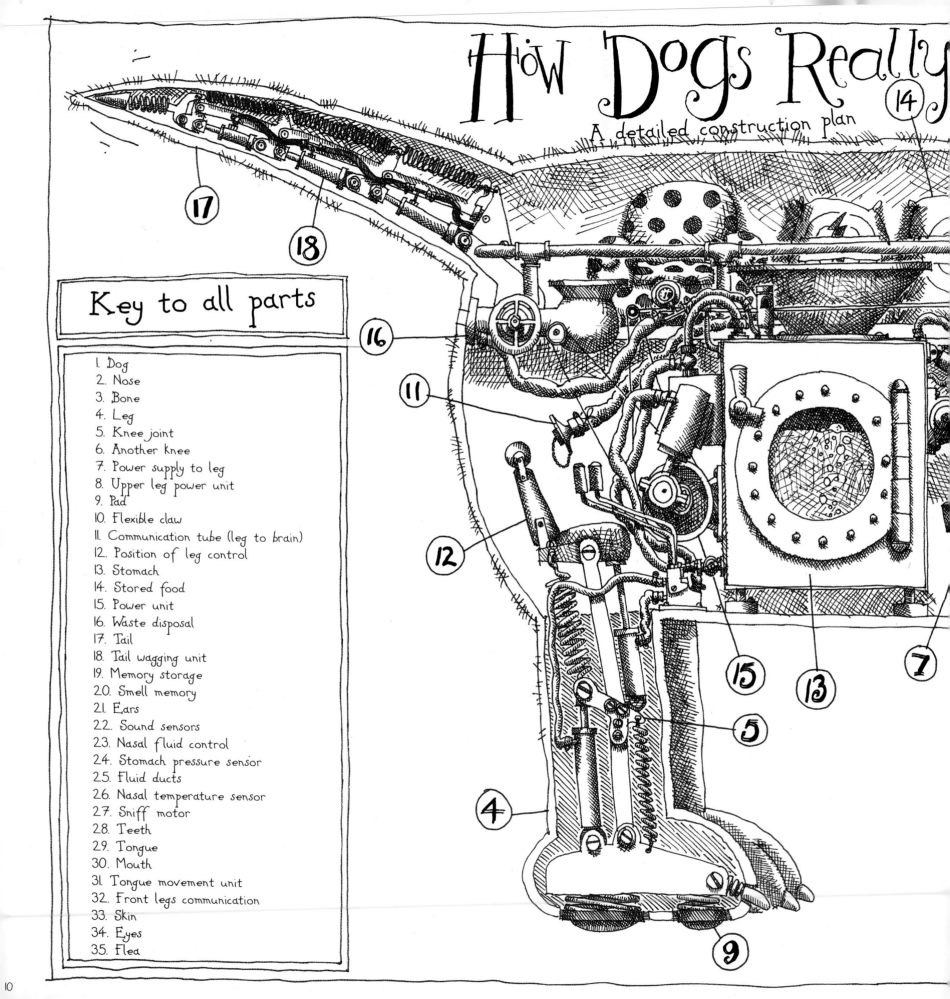

How Dogs Really

A detailed construction plan

Key to all parts

1. Dog
2. Nose
3. Bone
4. Leg
5. Knee joint
6. Another knee
7. Power supply to leg
8. Upper leg power unit
9. Pad
10. Flexible claw
11. Communication tube (leg to brain)
12. Position of leg control
13. Stomach
14. Stored food
15. Power unit
16. Waste disposal
17. Tail
18. Tail wagging unit
19. Memory storage
20. Smell memory
21. Ears
22. Sound sensors
23. Nasal fluid control
24. Stomach pressure sensor
25. Fluid ducts
26. Nasal temperature sensor
27. Sniff motor
28. Teeth
29. Tongue
30. Mouth
31. Tongue movement unit
32. Front legs communication
33. Skin
34. Eyes
35. Flea

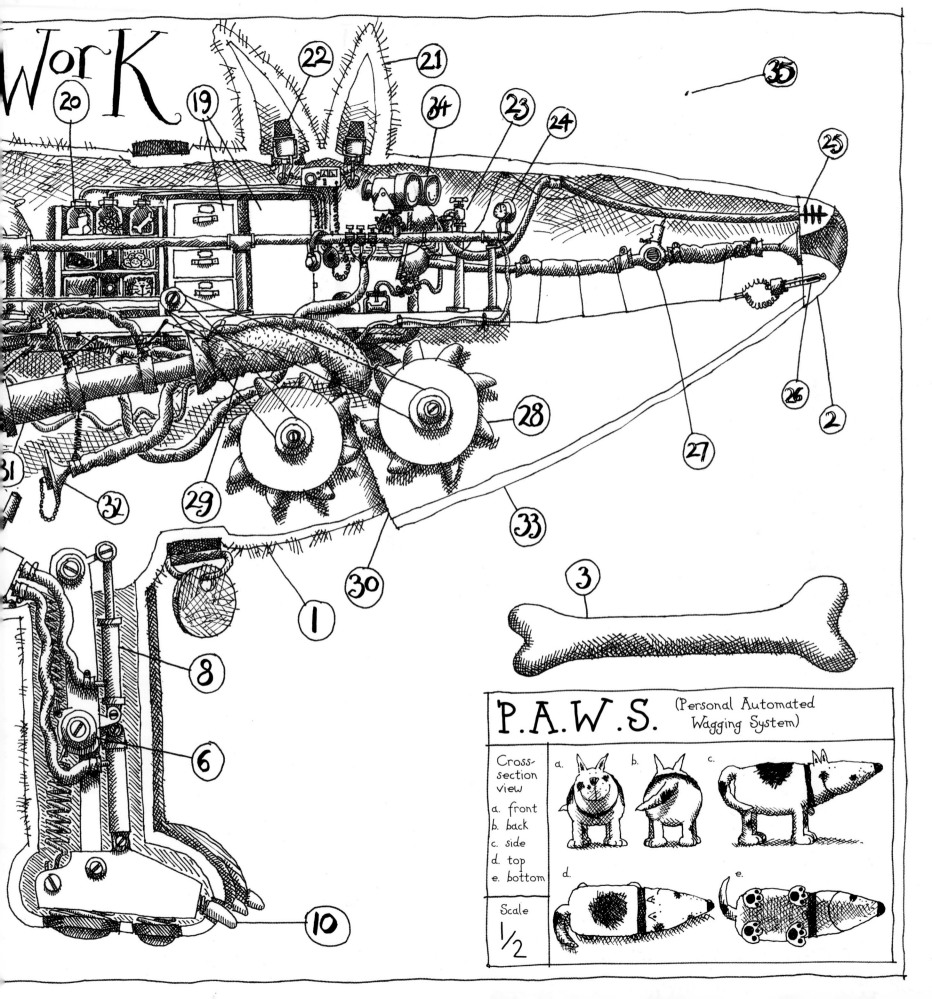

WorK

P.A.W.S. (Personal Automated Wagging System)

Cross-section view
a. front
b. back
c. side
d. top
e. bottom

Scale 1/2

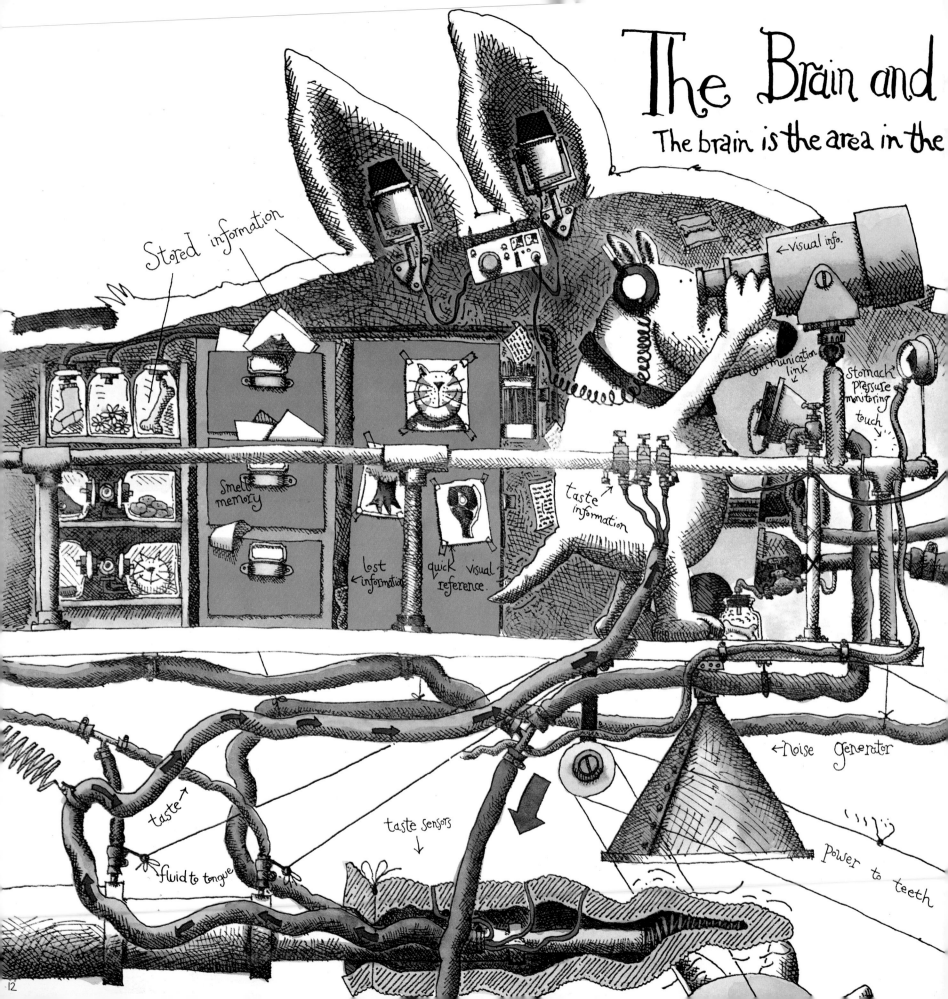

Stored information

← visual info.

communication link

stomach pressure monitoring touch

Smell memory

taste information

lost information

quick visual reference.

taste →

fluid to tongue

taste sensors ↓

← Noise generator

Power to teeth

12

Central Nervous System
head that controls the body!

All dogs, even the dull, boring ones, have some sort of brain. The brain receives information that comes from the senses (ears, eyes, nose, tongue, and touch sensors all over the body), and uses it to find food, cats, a place to sleep, and then more food. All the information that goes into the brain is compared with the information that is already there (called memories). The brain then decides what to do and sends out messages to the body. This results in a response. (See an example of a dog's brain in motion below.)

fluid distributor

←fluid

smells→

←smell

temperature sensor→

nostril.

touch sensors

teeth→

What happens
when a dog meets a cat

Dog thinks...

1. "What is this thing I see before me?"
2. "I saw one of these yesterday and it was as ugly then, as it is now."
3. "What shall I do? What did I do yesterday?"
4. "I shall bark at it, because I did that yesterday and it went off and left me to eat and sleep in peace."
5. Brain tells body to bark.
6. Cat runs off. 7. Dog goes to sleep.

①

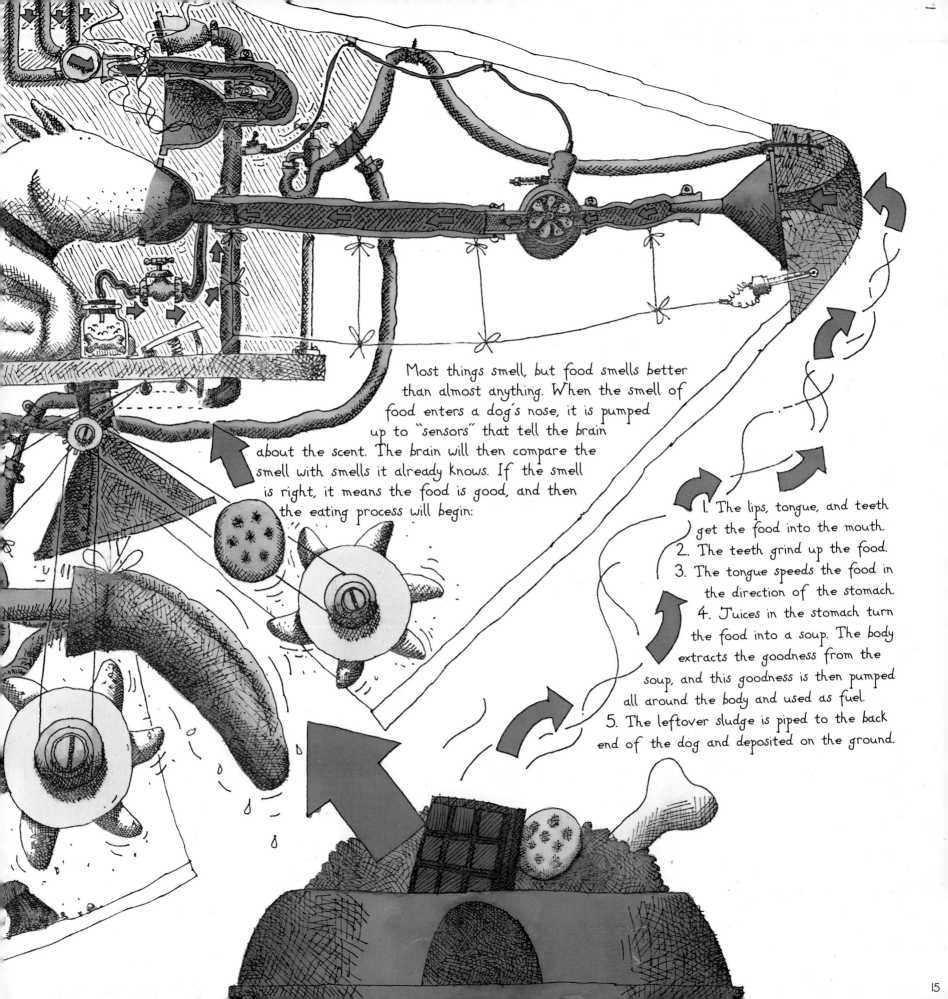

Most things smell, but food smells better than almost anything. When the smell of food enters a dog's nose, it is pumped up to "sensors" that tell the brain about the scent. The brain will then compare the smell with smells it already knows. If the smell is right, it means the food is good, and then the eating process will begin:

1. The lips, tongue, and teeth get the food into the mouth.
2. The teeth grind up the food.
3. The tongue speeds the food in the direction of the stomach.
4. Juices in the stomach turn the food into a soup. The body extracts the goodness from the soup, and this goodness is then pumped all around the body and used as fuel.
5. The leftover sludge is piped to the back end of the dog and deposited on the ground.

Communication

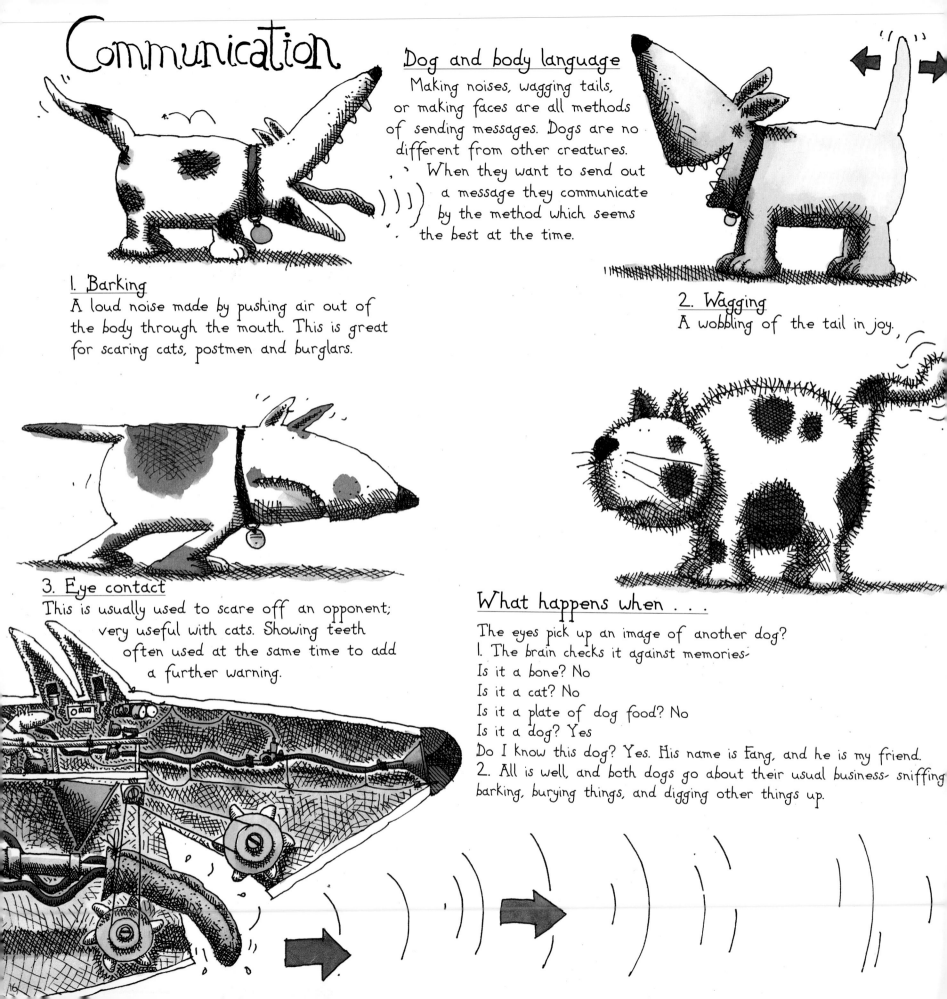

Dog and body language

Making noises, wagging tails, or making faces are all methods of sending messages. Dogs are no different from other creatures. When they want to send out a message they communicate by the method which seems the best at the time.

1. Barking
A loud noise made by pushing air out of the body through the mouth. This is great for scaring cats, postmen and burglars.

2. Wagging
A wobbling of the tail in joy.

3. Eye contact
This is usually used to scare off an opponent; very useful with cats. Showing teeth often used at the same time to add a further warning.

What happens when . . .

The eyes pick up an image of another dog?
1. The brain checks it against memories.
Is it a bone? No
Is it a cat? No
Is it a plate of dog food? No
Is it a dog? Yes
Do I know this dog? Yes. His name is Fang, and he is my friend.
2. All is well, and both dogs go about their usual business- sniffing barking, burying things, and digging other things up.

Dogs don't speak English!

You can make dogs understand a few simple words - such as "food," "walk," or "cat" - if you speak clearly and loudly. But no matter how clearly or loudly you speak, dogs will not understand "No!" or "These are not my slippers!" or even "If you do that again, I will not be a happy owner!"

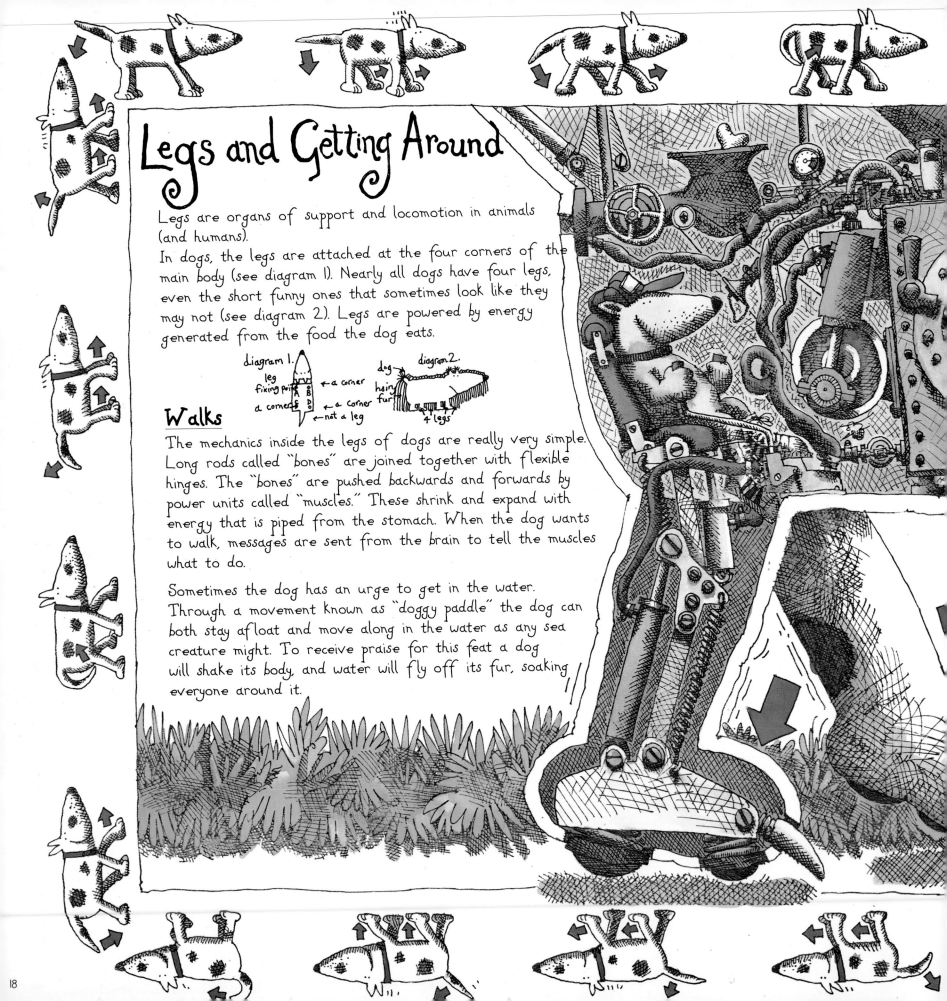

Legs and Getting Around

Legs are organs of support and locomotion in animals (and humans).

In dogs, the legs are attached at the four corners of the main body (see diagram 1). Nearly all dogs have four legs, even the short funny ones that sometimes look like they may not (see diagram 2). Legs are powered by energy generated from the food the dog eats.

diagram 1.
leg
fixing point
a corner
← a corner
← a corner
← not a leg

dog
diagram 2.
hair
fur
4 legs

Walks

The mechanics inside the legs of dogs are really very simple. Long rods called "bones" are joined together with flexible hinges. The "bones" are pushed backwards and forwards by power units called "muscles." These shrink and expand with energy that is piped from the stomach. When the dog wants to walk, messages are sent from the brain to tell the muscles what to do.

Sometimes the dog has an urge to get in the water. Through a movement known as "doggy paddle" the dog can both stay afloat and move along in the water as any sea creature might. To receive praise for this feat a dog will shake its body, and water will fly off its fur, soaking everyone around it.

The Family Tree

In the days before people started to keep dogs (when dogs were closer to their relatives-wolves, coyotes, dingos, and so on), dogs used to look after themselves. They lived in big family groups called packs. Since dogs always hang around where there is food, they sometimes came into contact with humans. Slowly some of them became friendly with the humans. As the dogs became pets, the humans slowly began to develop the dogs so they would be more useful, and as a result the dogs became more and more different...some had big noses, some long legs, and others short ears, but most of them were less and less like their great-great-great-grandparents....

DOGS AND OWNERS
Is there any difference?

It is often said that "dogs look like their owners!" This is the wrong way around. In fact an owner will slowly start to resemble his or her dog; the clues are easy to spot.

1. A boring dog will just do the same things all the time.
Result – A dull and boring owner.

2. A pretty pampered dog will make its owner feel ugly and inferior.
Result – The owner will rush off to the beauty salon.

3. A fat, lazy dog will not want to go for walks.
Result – the owner gets fat!

4. A smelly, scruffy dog will pollute its home.
Result – Keep away from this dog, its owner and their house.

5. An interesting and clever dog will drag its owner to many interesting and surprising places.
Result – An interesting and clever owner!

Do you know any dog owners? Are they like their pets?
Do you have a dog? Are you like it?

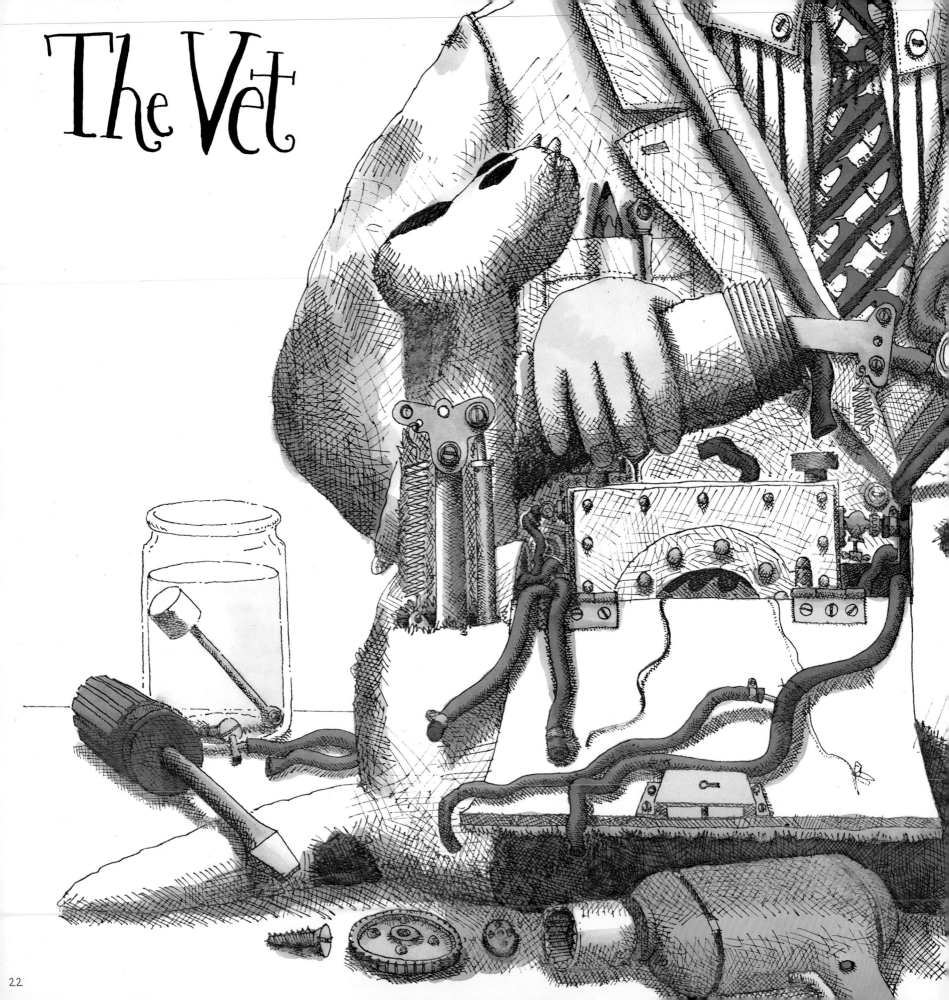

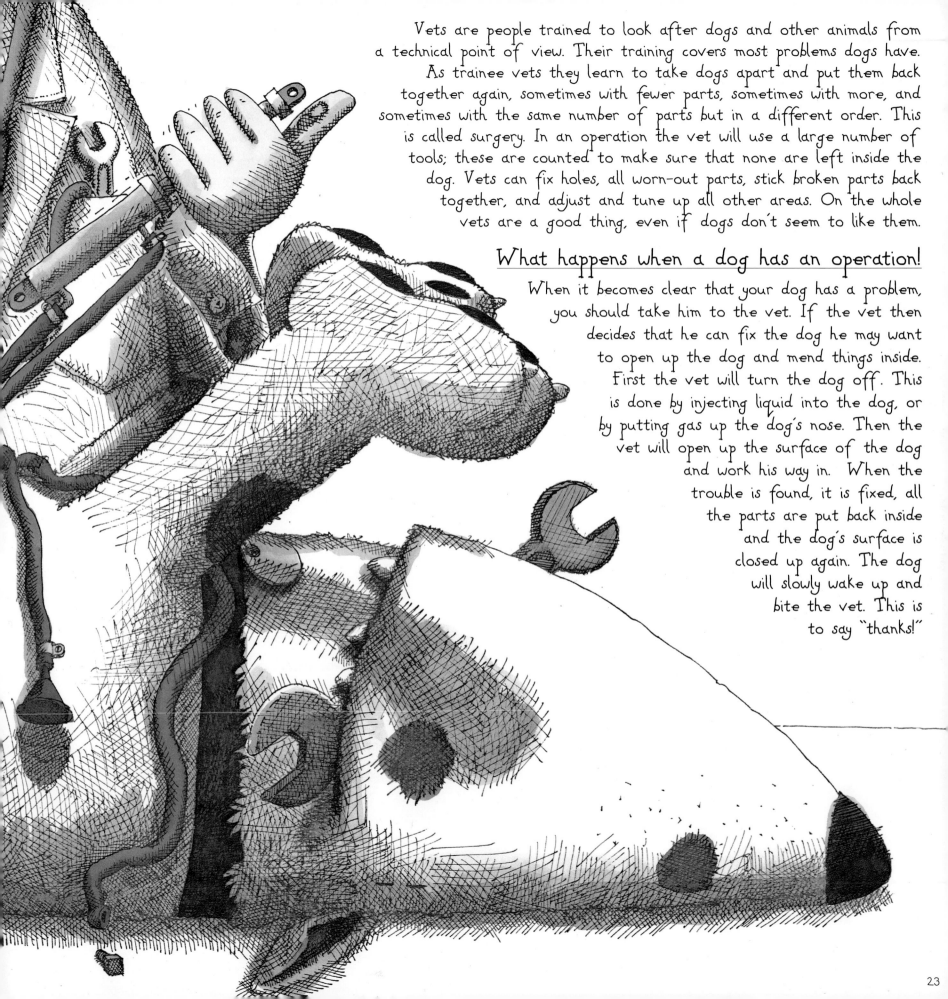

Vets are people trained to look after dogs and other animals from a technical point of view. Their training covers most problems dogs have. As trainee vets they learn to take dogs apart and put them back together again, sometimes with fewer parts, sometimes with more, and sometimes with the same number of parts but in a different order. This is called surgery. In an operation the vet will use a large number of tools; these are counted to make sure that none are left inside the dog. Vets can fix holes, all worn-out parts, stick broken parts back together, and adjust and tune up all other areas. On the whole vets are a good thing, even if dogs don't seem to like them.

What happens when a dog has an operation!

When it becomes clear that your dog has a problem, you should take him to the vet. If the vet then decides that he can fix the dog he may want to open up the dog and mend things inside. First the vet will turn the dog off. This is done by injecting liquid into the dog, or by putting gas up the dog's nose. Then the vet will open up the surface of the dog and work his way in. When the trouble is found, it is fixed, all the parts are put back inside and the dog's surface is closed up again. The dog will slowly wake up and bite the vet. This is to say "thanks!"

General Maintenance

(Warning...Dogs may be clever, but this will not stop them from getting very hungry if you don't feed them often enough.)

Dogs need fuel! It is what makes them go. If they do not get it they will stop. This is because fuel is turned into power, which in turn builds the materials to maintain, and even rebuild, their structures.

One should put the right amount of fuel into a dog. As they will eat almost anything put in front of them it is important to control the flow of food into their bodies. If the belly of the dog is rubbing on the floor you are probably overfeeding, unless your dog has very short legs. If your dog starts to try to open cans of food with his teeth, his food intake probably needs checking.

Make sure you are running your dog on the right fuel. If you are not it may affect the dog's performance.

This is not the right fuel.

Keeping your dog undercover at night will make it last longer and keep it in better condition. Failure to do so may badly affect the resale value of your dog.

Walks

It is a good thing to take your dog out for a run as this will keep him in first-rate working order. This should be once or twice a day. It is unlikely that you will be able to overexercise your dog once he is used to it. Take objects along to test his systems. You can test his retrieval mechanisms by throwing a ball or stick and seeing what happens. If the dog goes and gets it, this means all is well. If he does not, it may mean that:

1. You have thrown it into some prickers.
2. The dog is more interested in almost anything else.
3. He is a boring dog.
4. He is shortsighted.
5. You have forgotten to let go of the stick.

Maintenance chart

PROBLEM	CAUSE	HOW TO FIX:
GROWLING	BAD MANNERS OR REDUCED FOOD	THROW FOOD AT IT OR CHANGE DOG'S DIET
FAT + LAZY	OVERFEEDING	EXERCISE OR REDUCE INPUT OF FOOD
THIN + TIRED	OVEREXERCISE	FEED MORE

Given a large enough yard that is safe and secure, dogs can exercise themselves....

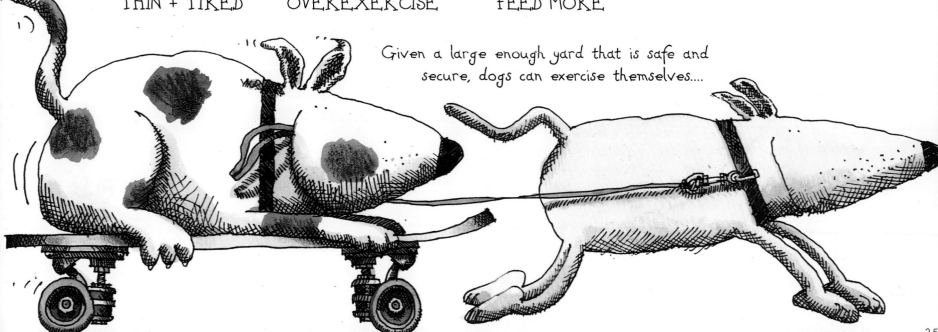

return to home environment

chase invaders

check responses

Dogs and Their Environment

Most dogs have an area that they live in; this is called a territory. Some share this area with either humans or other dogs, and sometimes even with a cat. This is not a happy state of affairs! A dog will mark out his territory and will guard it.

Chew bone for energy

Chase tail to check energy level

play with item

bury leftovers

The End

Index